OSPREYS

First published in Great Britain in 1991 by
Colin Baxter Photography Ltd.,
Unit 2/3, Block 6,
Caldwellside Industrial Estate,
LANARK, ML11 6SR

British Library Cataloguing in Publication Data
Dennis, Roy, 1940
    Ospreys.
    I. Title
    I. Falconiformes
    598.917

    ISBN 0-948661-19-4

Photographs by

Front Cover © Laurie Campbell
Back Cover © Laurie Campbell
Page 19 © Mike Read (Swift)
Page 20 © Juhani Koivu
Page 21 © John Shaw (NHPA)
Page 22 © Juhani Koivu
Page 23 © Juhani Koivu
Page 24 © C. H. Crooke
Page 25 © Roy Dennis
Page 26 © Roy Dennis
Page 27 © Colin Baxter
Page 28 Top © Roy Dennis
Page 28 Bottom © Roy Dennis
Page 29 © Juhani Koivu
Page 30 Illustration © Iain Sarjent

Page 35 © Roy Dennis
Page 36 © Juhani Koivu
Page 37 © Pekka Helo (Bruce Coleman)
Page 38 © Joe Van Wormer (Bruce Coleman)
Page 39 © Roy Dennis
Page 40 © Colin Baxter
Page 41 © Roy Dennis
Page 42 Top Left © Laurie Campbell
Page 42 Bottom Left © Laurie Campbell
Page 42 Top Right © Laurie Campbell
Page 42 Bottom Right © Laurie Campbell
Page 43 © Laurie Campbell
Page 44 © Gordon Langsbury (Bruce Coleman)
Page 45 © Laurie Campbell
Page 46 Illustration © Iain Sarjent

Osprey Illustration © Keith Brockie

Printed in Great Britain by
Frank Peters (Printers) Ltd., Kendal.

OSPREYS

Roy Dennis

Colin Baxter Photography Ltd., Lanark, Scotland

Ospreys

Like so many people in Britain I saw my first Osprey at Loch Garten in the Highlands of Scotland; that was thirty-one years ago. I can still remember the thrill of that first encounter despite the passage of time. It was the 8th of April 1960 and as newly appointed warden at the RSPB's Osprey reserve I was anxious for the return of Scotland's only breeding pair of Ospreys. The day was cold and grey and wet. My morning visit to the nest tree near Loch Garten had drawn a blank and I expected no better luck as the rain continued to fall after lunch. To me it was as if a shaft of sunlight had touched the nest tree as there, just two hundred yards across the forest bog, was my first ever Osprey. It was the male bird and he was a very damp looking Osprey as he perched quietly preening in the branches of the ancient Scots pine. He was very tired after his long migration and I watched him for several hours before he flew off to fish before dark. I got to know him well as we both waited ten more days until his mate flew in from Africa.

That year they reared two young Ospreys at Loch Garten and they also succeeded in hooking me as a lifelong enthusiast for a very special bird. Since then I have seen the population in Scotland gradually rise to over 60 pairs. I have followed them to their winter quarters in West Africa and I have seen their ancestors nesting among the lakes of Sweden. I have looked at nests on stunning pinnacles of rock on the sea coast of Corsica and on low trees in the salt marshes of New England. As I write on a snowy December evening it is easy for me to imagine our Ospreys roosting in the hot and humid mangrove swamps of Senegal and Gambia. In a couple of months' time they will set off north once again and I look forward to their return. To me they are the sign of spring in the Scottish Highlands.

The Osprey is a bird of prey specialising in catching fish. In Scotland, its Gaelic name, lasgair, means fisherman and in the past it was often referred to as the fish-hawk. It is a large raptor, nearly two feet in length with a wingspan of five feet. The upper parts are dark brown, but the feathers are tipped white when young. The underparts are white with a distinctive brown band across the breast which is thicker and darker on the female. The head is white with a dark brown stripe through the eye reaching to the back of the neck. The crested head is variably marked with brown. The long wings are white underneath marked with brown, while the tail is barred brown and buff, being paler in the male. The legs and feet are greenish-grey and powerful with long black talons; the outer toe is reversible allowing the Osprey to grip fish with two talons forward and two back. Further help is provided by the distinctively scaly or prickly skin on the feet. The strong black bill is noticeably hooked for tearing up fish. The eyes are bright yellow but more orange when juvenile. The call notes are a varied selection of whistles and squeals.

Ospreys occur throughout the world. They live in salt and freshwater habitats and they nest in trees as well as on rocks and on the ground. Most populations are migratory and the bulk of the world's estimated population of 25,000 to 30,000 pairs of Ospreys nest in the northern hemisphere and winter further south. There is only one species of Osprey in the world, and it is in a family of its own, the genus *Pandion* and the species *haliaetos. Pandion* comes from the name of a king in ancient Greece but the link is difficult to understand; *haliaetus* is more easily understood, *'hal'* denoting the sea or salt-water and *'aetus'* from the Greek word aetos for eagle. There are four subspecies of Ospreys in the world; the nominate *haliaetus* breeds in Europe, north Africa and northern Asia. *Carolinensis* breeds in North America; *ridgwayi* in the Caribbean and *cristatus* in Australasia. They vary slightly in size and coloration but all are instantly recognisable as typical Ospreys.

The past history of the Osprey in the British Isles is very sad. After centuries of persecution the last pair nested in 1916 in Inverness-shire. They were then extinct as a breeding species in our country until their return in 1954. In the Middle Ages the Osprey would have been well distributed throughout the British Isles nesting along sea coasts as well as by rivers and lakes. Various writers refer to the bird in the 16th and 17th centuries but soon after persecution began and reached a peak in the 18th and 19th centuries. The last pairs nested in Ireland in 1800 and in Somerset, England in 1842. Thereafter they were confined to Scotland.

Written records became more accurate in the last century so the sorry demise of the Osprey in Scotland is well-documented. There were probably 40-50 pairs remaining by 1850 and by this time their rarity added to their problems because the eggs and skins were collector's trophies. Today, the exploits of collectors like Charles St.John and William Dunbar in Sutherland make very disturbing reading, but in those days it was an acceptable activity of naturalists. They shot the adults and robbed the nests and in a few short years the Ospreys in north-west Sutherland were extinct. I find the stories even more poignant because I have seen the lochs and even the exact rocks where the Ospreys once nested so it is possible to imagine what it was like in the old days. On 17th May, 1848 St.John and Dunbar went to Loch an Laig Ard just north of Scourie. When they arrived they saw the white head of the female incubating her eggs in the eyrie on a rocky islet. While his friend went for the boat, St.John shot the female as she flew by. Soon after the male returned with a fish for his mate and St.John writes "that he flew around, plainly turning his head to the right and left, as if looking for her, and as if in astonishment at her unwonted absence". Soon after he took the two eggs from the nest and as he rowed away he recalls "the male bird unceasingly calling and seeking for his hen. I was really sorry I had shot her".

Meanwhile, in Strathspey Dunbar's brother Lewis was harrying the remaining Ospreys in that district. In 1851, he walked through the night to Loch an Eilein, near Aviemore, where Ospreys nested on the deserted castle on an island in the loch. At 3 am on 3rd May, he slipped into the icy waters and swam to the castle. It was snowing and his climb up the castle ramparts to the nest was hampered by six inches of snow. He took the two eggs and swam to the shore holding an egg in each hand. He blew the eggs in the boat-house and washed the insides with whisky. Like other eggs they were bought by collectors in the south.

Despite attempts to protect the few remaining pairs, especially by the Grants of Rothiemurchus at Loch an Eilein and by Cameron of Lochiel at Loch Arkaig, successful breeding was very rarely achieved. They reared two young at Loch an Eilein in 1896; they failed in the next three years and the single Osprey which returned to the eyrie in 1901 and 1902 was the last occupant of that famous nest. At the island on Loch Arkaig, near Fort William, Ospreys regularly nested there until 1908 when they last reared young. By this time, the nest had been placed under police protection with barbed wire defences. Sadly, only one bird was present in 1909 and returned unmated for the next four years; and thus another famous site was deserted. The last known pair nested at nearby Loch Loyne in 1916 after which the Osprey became extinct in Scotland. As William Dunbar wrote to the collector John Wooley: "I am afraid that Mr St.John, yourself and your humble servant have finally done for the Ospreys".

Elsewhere in Europe, they were also being persecuted and undoubtedly some of the last Scottish birds were shot on migration outside Scotland. In consequence migrant Ospreys became very rare in Scotland, although the occasional one was seen in their ancestral haunts and there was even an attempt to reintroduce Ospreys. Captain Knight, the celebrated bird-of-prey enthusiast, released four young American Ospreys at Loch Arkaig in 1929 but nothing came of this venture.

In the 1950s the numbers of breeding Ospreys in Scandinavia started to rise rapidly through increased protection and this would have been the origin of migrants seen in the Scottish Highlands. In fact, young Ospreys ringed in Sweden were recovered dead in the Highlands in 1949 and 1955. Three Ospreys were seen in Strathspey on 29th August 1953 but nesting was not proved until the following year when a pair reared two young, probably near Loch Garten. In 1955, they were back but the eggs were almost certainly stolen, as later in the season they were seen building a frustration nest some miles away. In 1956, they laid eggs at an eyrie in Rothiemurchus but again they were robbed and once more built a frustration eyrie. Despite the protective efforts of several Osprey enthusiasts over these years it was very disappointing that the nests continued to be pillaged.

In 1957, George Waterston, the Director of the Royal Society for the Protection of Birds in Scotland arranged for the Ospreys to be protected around the clock by wardens. Sadly, only one bird returned to the old eyrie near Loch Garten, and there were rumours another had been shot elsewhere in Strathspey. In 1958, the male returned on the first day of May to the nest on the south side of Loch Garten and was joined on the third day of May by a female. Operation Osprey, as the RSPB called their protection scheme, immediately swung into action. Just in time, as on the 11th May when the female laid her first egg a known egg collector was seen at the tree and chased off. A team of volunteers guarded the nest day and night but their efforts failed. On the 3rd of June another egg collector raided the nest on a very dark, rainy night. Two eggs were found smashed below the nest and two hen's eggs daubed with brown shoe polish were discovered in the nest. The thief was never traced. As before, the Ospreys built a frustration nest, this time on a tall Scots pine to the north of the loch.

This disaster made headline news and there was widespread concern that these magnificent birds should be harried just as they were in Victorian times. With the kind co-operation of the Countess of Seafield and her estate staff, the area around Loch Garten was declared a protected bird sanctuary in 1959 by the Secretary of State for Scotland. This made it an offence to enter the area near the nest without permission. The nest at the north side of Loch Garten was protected and an appeal by the RSPB resulted in a full complement of volunteers to watch over the Ospreys when they returned for the 1959 season. The male came back on the 18th April, the female on the 22nd and the first egg was laid on the 1st day of May. By the 8th June, there were definitely young in the nest and soon after the successful hatch George Waterston made a brave and, in retrospect, very far-sighted decision to open the observation post to allow the general public to see the Ospreys and their young. In the seven weeks until the young flew 14,000 people came to view the birds. It was an outstanding success for the Ospreys, the public and conservation.

Each year since, Ospreys have returned to Loch Garten and it has become world famous. The arrival of the birds and their fortunes have been eagerly followed by the press, radio and television. They have become one of the Highland's premier tourist attractions and nearly one and a half million people have visited the site in the last three decades. Hundreds of volunteers have helped the RSPB maintain Operation Osprey and a succession of staff have worked at Loch Garten. Operation Osprey was helped greatly by local people in the early years and now it is an accepted part of Strathspey life. In 1975 the Society purchased the forest around Loch Garten as a nature reserve which has steadily increased over the years until now the Abernethy Forest nature reserve extends to 30,000 acres and protects the future of the ancient pine forest and its special flora and fauna, including the Ospreys. I always find it salutary to remember that it all started with just one pair of Ospreys choosing Loch Garten as their first nesting place.

I was warden at Loch Garten from 1960 to 1963; in the first three years they reared two, three and one young respectively but in the last year the nest and eggs were destroyed in a gale; the same fate occurred in 1966. In 1971 the nest was again raided by vandals and the eggs stolen. The culprits were fined at Inverness Sheriff Court. In 1975 and 1985-87 the birds failed from natural causes. Over the years, a grand total of 58 young have been reared at Loch Garten. Sadly, the successes have been marred by vandalism - twice the nest tree has been damaged and at the time of writing arsonists have burnt down the observation post. How appalling that a few people will go to such lengths to destroy Osprey eggs for their illegal pleasures and then take such acts of revenge against the RSPB who try to prevent the robberies and give so much enjoyment to visitors to Loch Garten.

In 1963, a second pair of Ospreys became established near Aviemore and three years later the population rose to three pairs. From then on there has been a steady increase with seven pairs rearing eleven young in 1970. Numbers reached 20 pairs in 1977, 30 pairs in 1982, 42 pairs in 1986, 50 pairs in 1987 and 62 pairs in 1990. The Ospreys have of course moved outwith Strathspey and now occupy many parts of Scotland, where they have been welcomed and looked after by many people - landowners, gamekeepers, farmers, foresters and naturalists. RSPB staff have annually monitored the Scottish Ospreys as well as assisting their successful colonisation. By the end of 1990, at least 836 young Ospreys have flown from Scottish nests since 1954. The next milestones will be 100 young fledged in one year and then 100 pairs nesting in one year. Both of these targets should be reached well before the start of the next century. One day, Ospreys should return to their ancestral haunts in north-west Sutherland and even to England, Wales and Ireland.

Scotland is often still cold and wintry when the first Ospreys return from Africa. I usually see my first bird in the last week of March. It is never really dramatic, usually a tired bird perched on or beside its previous year's eyrie - but it is always a great thrill for me. Most return in the first half of April. The mean date of return at Loch Garten for males is 9th April, range 27th March - 22nd April, and for females 10th April, range 28th March - 26th April. In 16 years the male arrived before the female, 12 times the female was first and twice they arrived on the same day. Overall well-established birds arrive earlier and there is some indication that particular birds are regularly early or late arrivers. If both birds have survived the winter and the return migration, they usually pair up again for another season. Younger birds breeding for the first time arrive later and non-breeding birds continue to arrive well into May. Ospreys start to breed for the first time when three to five years old.

The display of the male Osprey is a most beautiful spectacle although often difficult for us to observe. After catching a fish, he gains height as he returns to the nesting area and while still several kilometres away he starts his display. To me the display call is very distinctive; it's a high-pitched 'pee-pee-pee-pee...pee' and if I search the skies I will see him soaring majestically, maybe a thousand feet above, as he moves in sweeping circles closer and closer to the nesting site. He climbs several hundred feet upwards with rapidly beating wings, then hovering briefly, with fanned tail, he performs a breathtaking dive showing the fish grasped in outstretched talons. He pulls out of the dive and powers sky-wards to repeat the performance. All the time his calling can be heard by his mate and finally his last stoop takes him in a long power dive right to the eyrie, where the fish is presented to his mate.

Most eyries survive the winter, especially larger well-established nests, but sometimes nests are destroyed in winter storms and this means complete re-building in the spring. Usually, all the birds must do is refurbish the old nest. As soon as they return they start to add dead sticks to the nest. The male tends to bring in larger sticks and the female more moss, bark and grass to line the nest. Old established eyries may be over a metre deep and just as wide. They are always built in the very top of a tree. In Scotland, most nests (70%) are built in Scots pines, with twice as many being in live trees than dead. Eyries have also been built in Douglas, Noble and silver firs, larch, Norway spruce, birch and oak. Within a week or so, their nest is ready and they scrape out a hollow in the centre in which to lay the eggs.

When young Ospreys return to Scotland to breed, having spent the previous summer looking round the breeding areas, they prefer to take over an established eyrie and will often pair up with a bird which has lost its mate. Some young pairs try to take over nests from established pairs and occasionally they are successful. Others may find an unused eyrie but most will have to establish their own territory and build a new nest, although many fail to complete it in time to breed successfully. The next year they should have better luck.

Mating is frequent at this time and usually in late April the female starts to lay her eggs. Early birds have laid from 14th April and late ones not until the 23rd May. The female does not leave the nesting area once the male is present and he provides her with fish; as egg-laying gets close she spends more time at the nest. She may roost on the eyrie the day before egg-laying and starts to incubate once she has laid the first egg. Normally, three beautifully blotched reddish-brown eggs are produced at two day intervals. First time breeders usually lay two eggs; single eggs are very rarely recorded and on three occasions in recent years a clutch of four eggs has been recorded.

Life at the eyrie now becomes very routine; the female sits throughout the night, the male roosting in a nearby tree. In the early morning, he sets off to hunt and when he returns with a fish, takes it to a favourite perch where he proceeds to devour the front half of the fish. After half an hour or so, the female starts to call peevishly and the male takes the remainder of the fish to the nest. She in turn takes it to her favourite perch while the male starts his longest daily spell of incubation. After feeding, the female preens, flies around but does not leave the vicinity. She often takes nest material back to the eyrie when she relieves her mate. During the day they may change over a few times and often in the early evening he will bring in another fish. Otherwise, incubation is quiet - it may be hot in the midday sun with the female panting on the nest, or it may be snowing or blowing a gale. Intruding Ospreys may call by and occasionally even try to steal the nest; a few times I have seen an eagle or peregrine pass by and the male noisily dive-bombs them on their way. But more disastrous by far is for their dawn to be shattered by the arrival of human egg thieves. The warm eggs are quickly removed and the men run off. When the female at last feels safe to return to her nest it is empty. Her whole cycle is broken and she does not know what to do. After a day the pair start to lose interest in the nest and their season is lost. Only exceptionally will they relay and try again.

The chicks cheep to their parents from within the egg and finally hatch out of their shells at thirty-five days. Taking nearly a day to break out, the whole clutch takes several days to hatch completely. Suddenly, the adults' behaviour changes - now when the male brings fish to the nest the female does not leave but carefully feeds tiny pieces of fresh fish to her young. Newly hatched chicks are helpless little creatures covered in brown and buff down. The female broods them continuously and feeds them several times a day. After about two weeks they are big enough to look over the edge of the nest and are growing rapidly. The male increases his fishing trips and by a month old they are eating about six fish a day. It is rare to see sibling aggression with Ospreys and nearly always the whole brood thrives. At a month, the young are very active; preening and starting to flap their growing wings. The female spends more time perched in the next door trees when the chicks are six weeks old, as they vigorously exercise their wings. Soon they lift a few inches above the nest, then a few feet and finally they are flying after about 52 days in the nest.

For the first couple of weeks the young continue to come to the nest for food brought in by the male, though rarely by the female. They spend much time chasing and playing near the nest trees, strengthening their wings for the long journey south. Before that they start to learn to fish in nearby waters, returning to feed at home if they fail.

They either fish from a hovering flight over the water or less commonly from a perch overlooking the water. Once a fish is sighted the bird starts to drop like a stone, the wings swept back and at the last moment the talons are thrust forwards and the bird grabs the fish under the surface of the water. Sometimes the whole bird is submerged. Experienced birds catch about once out of four dives but young birds make many attempts. Once a fish is caught, the Osprey rises out of the water, flapping its long wings strongly. The grip on the fish is secured and the final act before setting off homewards is for the Osprey to give itself a good shake in flight to shed the water.

They are equally at home along the coasts as beside lochs and rivers, in fact estuaries provide some of the richest feeding grounds. In Scotland they feed on a range of fish, with pike, trout and flounders being the principal prey, usually in the 500 gram range. Other species eaten include perch, sea trout, mullet and eel but there is not the wide variety of fish species available as in mainland Europe. They may at times conflict with man, principally at fish farms. In the early days, fish farmers were excited when they first had an Osprey visit but if it became regular their enthusiasm for this expert fisherman would wear off. They can be effectively kept out of fish farms by netting and it is more effective if the netting is erected over the ponds before they are stocked. Occasional wires or inefficient netting are dangerous as Ospreys may dive into the ponds and get entangled and die. Fortunately, salmon are either too small on their way to the sea or too big on their way back, so they do not feature in the Osprey's diet. Those trout that are taken are surely made up for by the spectacle of a fishing Osprey.

Over the years, we have ringed nearly 600 young Ospreys in Scotland and this has taught us much about their lives and migrations. At the end of August, most of our birds have set off south. Travelling independently and not as a family they take various routes. In September 1989, two young who had left the Highlands in August were identified by their colour rings by bird-watchers in Brittany while the following September, another young bird was recognised in South Wales. Recoveries of our birds show that they pass through Spain and Portugal, cross into North Africa and so down to their wintering quarters in West Africa. The first birds reach Senegal and Gambia in early October and they spend the winter fishing in the mangrove swamps and coastal waters. Fish, including flying fish, are abundant and the Osprey's life appears idyllic along the tropical shores of Africa. One sometimes wonders why they return to cold, snowy Scotland but the call of home is very strong.

On migration and in winter, they meet many other Ospreys from the larger breeding populations in Sweden and they may even meet the few resident birds which breed in the Mediterranean. The adults start to move north again in March and now there is no time to linger. Their ancient instincts drive them north and at this time of year they can run into bad weather which may delay them or even drive them off course, sometimes to their death. Two of our birds missed Scotland and ended up in the Faeroes and off Iceland. The latter bird was reared in the Highlands in 1976 and two years later it landed on a fishing boat north-west of Iceland in late April. The fishermen fed it and sent it to Reykjavik where the Museum Director arranged for the RSPB to collect the Osprey from Glasgow airport courtesy of Icelandair. Sadly, quarantine regulations prevented this and it had to be released in Iceland where, alas, it was found shot a month later.

The colour rings allow me to identify birds as individuals. My favourite Osprey is red Z; I ringed her as a chick in 1974 and she started to breed at nest 18 in 1980. In 1982, she became entangled in baler twine that she had collected from the farm fields as nest lining. After two days, she was still trailing the twine and I was worried she would get snagged in the branches so we set a trap in her nest. Once caught, I cut away the twine and released her back to incubate her eggs. In 1990, she returned once again to breed, in her sixteenth year, with her faithful mate who is twenty years old - our oldest Osprey. During their years together they have reared 24 young and are the most successful pair to date.

As the years go by we learn more about Ospreys; we see pairs establish themselves in new areas and we see old favourites disappear. The most noticeable change is that Ospreys can now be seen in many parts of Scotland and the thrill of seeing an Osprey catch a fish is available to many people. The bird is now secure in our country and it is just a shame that the stalwarts, like George Waterston, who nurtured those first prospecting birds in the early fifties are no longer with us to enjoy the success of their efforts.

Ospreys are specially adapted for catching fish and have keen eyesight.
Hovering several hundred feet above the water they dive
headlong to grab their prey. If successful they rise
slowly from the water grasping the wriggling fish.

Early spring is a busy time at the old eyrie as the birds repair the nest
after the winter storms. The female stands guard while the
male is away fishing. Mating takes place on the eyrie.

Ospreys usually lay beautifully marked eggs in the central cup of their
large nest. In this nest two eggs are normal colour while
the third is an unusual reddish variant.

In late April and early May, the female lays her eggs over a
period of a week. She starts incubation with the first egg.
Several times a day the male takes over incubation and
she perches in a nearby tree to eat, preen or rest.

Ospreys often nest in old dead trees in pine forests. Their nesting
sites may be inland beside lochs and rivers but they are also
at home near estuaries and coastal bays.

The first of the brood has just broken out of its egg.

Once the young Ospreys are well feathered, the female
often takes a break in the next door tree.

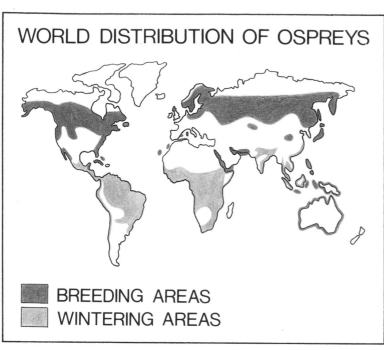

WORLD DISTRIBUTION OF OSPREYS

BREEDING AREAS
WINTERING AREAS

● RECOVERED WITHIN 1 YEAR

○ OLDER RECOVERIES
MARCH - AUGUST

● OLDER RECOVERIES
SEPTEMBER - FEBRUARY

RECOVERIES OF OSPREYS RINGED IN SCOTLAND

Osprey Conservation

Scottish Ospreys are doing well but they could do better. Of course they have a long way to go until you could say that they are either secure or have returned to the numbers which were present before persecution. The population has risen from one pair to over 60 pairs in three decades and future population growth depends on the output of young, their survival until breeding age, the age at which they first breed, their ability to locate new nesting areas and the longevity of breeders.

Over the last decade the annual production of young Ospreys in Scotland has been 1.44 young per active nest. Clearly, the numbers of young surviving to breeding age is greater than the loss of breeding adults and the population has increased. Studies abroad suggest a production of 0.8-1.0 young per nest is sufficient to maintain the population. About 40% of fledged young may return to breed, the rest being lost during their growing up years, especially the first migration and winter when they are most inexperienced and vulnerable. Out of 36 recoveries of Scottish ringed young found dead abroad, 22 of them were younger than one year old. Once they are established as breeders their chances of survival from one year to the next are as high as 90%.

We do not know how many pairs of Ospreys nested in Scotland before they were persecuted. From experience gathered from other countries and from examining the present situation in Scotland, I could envisage the Scottish population as between 500 and 1000 pairs, and the British population proportionately higher. We are used to seeing low numbers of birds of prey because our generation has seen the drastic results of centuries of persecution. For the population to recover fully, Ospreys need to recolonise the rest of the country. Ospreys get on surprisingly well with man, if left alone. In North America, Ospreys nest very close to people, in fact they are encouraged to nest close to houses so that people can enjoy the comings and goings at the eyrie.

What are the threats to our Ospreys and how do they die? Shooting and trapping was the usual end for many Ospreys in Europe in the earlier part of this century. The situation has now changed and in many countries where they were once victimised, they are now unmolested. The Scottish birds migrate down through Britain, France and Iberia and so on to West Africa. Of the 14 birds reported dead before 1980, at least 9 (64%) had been directly shot or killed by man, but since then only 5 (22%) out of 23 have been shot. In recent times the principal cause of death is collision with overhead wires (8 birds). Electricity power lines often cross estuaries, rivers and lakes on the Ospreys' migration routes so young birds are at great risk.

The Osprey is at the top of the aquatic food chain so breeding success and survival can be harmed by toxic chemicals. In North America there was catastrophic breeding failure and consequent population decline from 1950 due to DDT. Controls on its use resulted in recovery of the population and nesting success since 1970. In Scotland we did not have many Ospreys to be affected but some of the early pairs did suffer from egg-failures and traces of toxic chemicals were identified in eggs which failed to hatch. Other contaminants including dieldrin, mercury and PCBs have been identified in eggs but in Scotland none of these have occurred in high levels. Pesticide use is much lower nowadays in Britain but there have been increases in Africa, where our birds winter, but this has not shown up as a problem so far.

Overfishing or the loss of fish stocks through ecological damage could harm Ospreys but we do not know if this is a problem yet. The failure of

Ospreys to recolonise north-west Sutherland may be due to the present-day lack of fish in some lochs. The possible effects of acid rain and extensive conifer plantations may also affect them locally. Some pairs have failed due to a shortage of fish, exacerbated by bad weather. In fact, weather can be an important cause of mortality both for young in the nest and for birds on migration. It can also cause pairs to fail when storms blow down nests containing eggs or young; old established nests are rarely damaged but new nests built by young pairs sometimes come to grief.

In Scotland, where the population is small, human disturbance can still be a problem. Nests have failed during incubation due to accidental disturbance caused by unexpected hazards such as tree planters and motor bike rallies. A few nests have also failed due to over enthusiastic bird photographers keeping incubating birds off their nests. It is illegal to intentionally disturb these birds at their nests and if the birds are calling and not incubating, then people are too close.

The main cause of nest failure in Scotland is theft of eggs by vandals. Egg collectors were one of the main threats to the Victorian Ospreys and sometimes one wonders if we have changed all that much. In 1988, 11 out of 49 nests were robbed and the same fate befell 9 out of 49 nests in 1989. These activities are illegal and nowadays the penalty for stealing an Osprey's egg is as high as £2,000 per egg. Despite this, a small group of people annually break the law and destroy Ospreys' eggs in order to have blown shells in a hidden collection. At one nest in 1990 they even took the eggs the day before the first egg was due to hatch; their activities are destroying precious wildlife. The police and the RSPB endeavour to prevent these thefts but it is impossible to guard every nest for the whole five weeks of incubation. The loss of nests in recent years has amounted to 20% and if these had not been robbed it would have meant that about 200 young Ospreys instead of 162 young would have fledged in the two years of 1988 and 1989. In the future that will mean that only 60 instead of 80 young adults will return to Scotland to breed. This is a serious loss.

Young Ospreys are rather conservative and prefer to breed in areas where Ospreys have already settled and many prefer to return to their natal areas. Long ago when Ospreys nested throughout Britain they would have felt at home in places they shun at the present time. To overcome this problem, as well as disturbance and storm damage, we have, over the years, embarked on a programme of building artificial eyries to encourage Ospreys to nest in new areas. This has proved very successful and has resulted in young pairs breeding at the first opportunity and more successfully because their nests do not blow down. The fastest occupation I can remember was constructing a nest in a new area and having eggs laid in it five days later Nowadays, the nests are built to resemble natural nests as closely as possible, but Ospreys will take to nests in quiet man-made sites such as power pylons in Germany and harbour navigation posts in North America.

The future for Ospreys looks good but there is a long way to go until the species is back to full strength in Britain and the rest of southern Europe. Let us hope that the loss of eggs in Scotland ceases and that people leave them alone and accept them as neighbours to be enjoyed but not harried. They are beautiful birds. To watch an Osprey catch a fish is a thrilling sight, no matter how many times you have seen it before, and they are now once more a real harbinger of spring in Scotland.

Life can be wet and windy in the tree-top eyrie. The female tries to keep
her young warm; she and one of the young are very wet, their
backs covered with rain drops. On other days, the chicks
are warm and dry and growing fast.

Even when the young are well-grown the female will feed them. Tearing up the fish, she feeds each young with small pieces of flesh. Young Ospreys have orange eyes which turn pale yellow when adult.

A brood of young huddle together in their nest.

Beautiful Loch Garten is famous for Ospreys. In early July, young
Ospreys are ringed in Scotland as part of the conservation
study into their lives and migration.

Successful fishermen ready to head for home.

This young Osprey is fully grown and well-fed. Any day in
late summer he will set off to Africa.

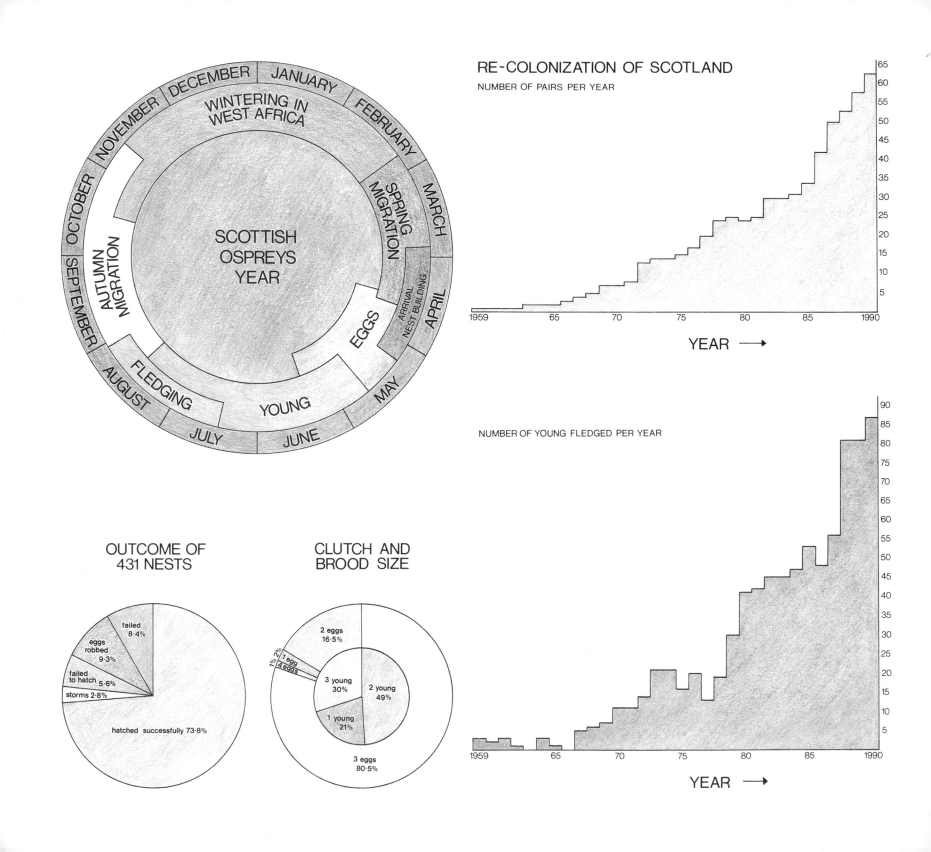

SCOTTISH OSPREYS YEAR

WINTERING IN WEST AFRICA

JANUARY · FEBRUARY · MARCH · APRIL · MAY · JUNE · JULY · AUGUST · SEPTEMBER · OCTOBER · NOVEMBER · DECEMBER

SPRING MIGRATION

AUTUMN MIGRATION

ARRIVAL NEST BUILDING

EGGS

YOUNG

FLEDGING

RE-COLONIZATION OF SCOTLAND

NUMBER OF PAIRS PER YEAR

YEAR ⟶

NUMBER OF YOUNG FLEDGED PER YEAR

YEAR ⟶

OUTCOME OF 431 NESTS

failed 8·4%

eggs robbed 9·3%

failed to hatch 5·6%

storms 2·8%

hatched successfully 73·8%

CLUTCH AND BROOD SIZE

2 eggs 16·5%

1% 2%

1 egg 4 eggs

3 eggs 80·5%

3 young 30%

1 young 21%

2 young 49%

Enjoying Ospreys

The best place in the British Isles to see Ospreys is at Loch Garten in the Scottish Highlands, where the Royal Society for the Protection of Birds have their famous Osprey observation post. As long as a pair of birds are in residence, usually from April to August, the RSPB welcome people to come and see the birds at their nest. Loch Garten is within the Society's Abernethy Forest reserve between Aviemore and Grantown-on-Spey in Badenoch & Strathspey. Best approach is via Boat-of-Garten or via Nethybridge if approaching from the east. It is well-signposted. There is a large car park by the loch and a pathway walk of 200 metres to the observation post, which is open from 9 am to 8.30 pm. There is a small admission charge (free to RSPB members); the observation post overlooks the nesting area; fixed telescopes and binoculars give an excellent view of the birds at the nest and the RSPB now provide a live video link from the nest which gives superb close-up views. There are information displays about Ospreys, an RSPB shop and wardens to assist.

The observation post is opened by the RSPB as soon as the birds have settled down in April. The latest information is available at the car park or by telephone from the RSPB. Usually there are incubating birds in late April and May with most activity when the male brings in fish, about twice a day. Chicks are in the eyrie in June and July, this being the busiest time at the nest. Depending on the state of the season flying young may be out of view later in August.

Fishing Ospreys are more difficult to observe; Loch Garten itself is poor for fish so the bird is rarely seen fishing there. In Strathspey birds fish on the river Spey as well as many other lochs; a visit to the fish farm at Aviemore which is open for visitors to observe rainbow trout may occasionally coincide with an Osprey hunting over the big fishing pond.

Nowadays, Ospreys can be seen throughout Scotland and a visit to any loch or part of the coastline may give a view of a fishing Osprey. In the past, they nested at the Scottish Wildlife Trust reserve near Dunkeld, Perthshire. If they return to the old eyrie, the visitor centre there will again give good views of the bird. If you come across other nests, please treat them with respect. If the birds are calling then you are too close; in the past this has caused Ospreys to break their eggs or desert their nests. It is illegal to intentionally disturb these rare birds at their nest. For the safety of the birds do not publicise the location of other nests; if you think you have found a previously unknown nest the RSPB would like to know for the purposes of monitoring and protecting the population.

Osprey Facts

Other Names:

Gaelic - Iasgair	**Swedish** - Fiskgjuse
German - Fischadler	**Finnish** - Saaksi
Russian - Ckona	**French** - Balbuzard pecheur
Dutch - Visarend	**Spanish** - Aguila pescadora
Danish - Fiskeorn	**Italian** - Falco pescatore

Scientific name: *Pandion haliaetus*

Races or sub-species:

P.h.haliaetus: Europe, Asia, North Africa
P.h.cristatus: Australia, South-east Asia
P.h.carolinensis: North America
P.h.ridgwayi: Caribbean

Breeding population:

Scotland	62 pairs (1990)
Scandinavia	ca 3,000 pairs
Europe (S & W)	100 pairs
World	ca 25,000-30,000 pairs

Measurements (average for haliaetus):

	male	female
Length (cms)	56-60	57-62
Wingspan (cms)	147-166	154-170
Tail (cms)	19-21	20-23
Weight (gms)	1,400	1,600

Breeding:

Age at first breeding 3-5 years
Single-brooded

Clutch size: 3, sometimes 2, rare 4

Egg size: (mms) 62 x 46

Fresh weight of egg: 72 gms

Incubation period: 35 days
Both incubate, mainly female

Fledging period: 53 days

Plumage characteristics:

First down plumage at hatching
Second down from 11 days
First complete feathers 42 days
Full adult plumage 18 months

Recommended Reading

Ospreys: A Natural and Unnatural History by Alan Poole, published by Cambridge University Press, 1989 is the best scientific book on the Osprey throughout the world and a very interesting read. Two older books available from libraries detail the past history of Ospreys in Scotland; they are *The Return of the Osprey* by Philip Brown & George Waterston, Collins 1962 and *The Scottish Ospreys* by Philip Brown, Heinneman 1979.

Biographical Note

Roy Dennis is a professional ornithologist living near Loch Garten in the Scottish Highlands. For 8 years in the 1960s, he and his wife ran the Bird Observatory on Fair Isle, famous for bird migration and seabirds. From 1971 to 1990, he was the RSPB's senior officer in the Highlands and is now a self-employed wildlife consultant. He has studied Ospreys in Scotland since 1960 and has seen them in many countries while studying birds throughout the world. He is a well-known lecturer, broadcaster and writer.